M000274073

live today well
COLLECTIVE

ISBN 978-0999277331

www.livetodaywellco.com

SEEK

a journal for exploring God's extraordinary love

K. Becker & M. Williams
2018

CONTENTS
of this journal

Hear, O Lord,
when I cry aloud,
be gracious to me and
answer me!
Come, my heart says,
seek his face!
Your face, Lord,
do I seek.
Do not hide
your face from me.

Psalm 27:7-9

INTRODUCTION

Scripture tells us that we are made in the image of God. We are each purposefully created for a deeply intimate relationship with the Divine. He seeks us daily, pursuing us through the humble and beautiful ordinary moments of our everyday lives.

Just as we can fall prey to comparing ourselves to others in this age of social media, as Christians, we are easily prone to comparing our spiritual lives to those of the saints.

At times it can be a struggle to relate to our spiritual heroes and the seemingly deep and mysterious connections that they appear to possess with God. They prayed big and they lived big; they did amazing things for God's glory. In comparison, what have we done today? Perhaps we folded a load of laundry, drove through rush hour traffic, made dinner for our loved ones, or washed the kitchen floor. Sometimes it doesn't feel like we're doing, seeing, or experiencing enough for God.

Yet, God tells us that we are each loved and we are each called to be holy. He invites each of us to play a valuable and irreplaceable role in the Kingdom of God. Holiness doesn't always mean completing the biggest task possible. Instead, simple holiness means embracing His love for us and sharing it with others through the way we live our lives.

God extends the gift of His love to us in the seemingly mundane experiences of daily life. All that He asks of us is that we gaze upon each ordinary moment with the eyes of our hearts long enough to see His extraordinary love and return it wholeheartedly.

What is the purpose of the Seek Journal?

The purpose of the Seek Journal is to help you to recognize God's presence in your day to day life and enter into a deeper relationship with the One who has loved you into being since the beginning.

Our faith isn't comprised merely of the words that we pray on Sundays, though those are fundamentally important, too. Our faith is also an action; we are called to live our faith out each and every day. At the end of Mass, we are commissioned to "go in peace to love and serve the Lord." We are encouraged to become what we repeatedly do. Spiritual practices help us do just that in our everyday lives.

What is a spiritual practice?

Spiritual practices are consciously chosen habits or rhythms that help us to enter more deeply into prayer and to more fully live out our faith. While there are many spiritual practices that have been well defined and used throughout history (for example, Lectio Divina or the Ignatian Examen), there is no wrong way to pray. What matters most is the orientation of the heart and openness to Him. Each of us are invited to explore different spiritual practices and use the ones that will most deepen our relationship with God.

This humble journal is meant to assist you in cultivating the spiritual practice of recognizing the extraordinarily intimate love of God in the everyday, ordinary moments of your life. The more that you pray with the Seek Journal and reflect on God's presence and movement in your life, the easier it will be to cultivate a heart of gratitude and live out each day with humble holiness.

How do I use the Seek Journal?

This journal poses reflective questions to help you meditate on a specific moment in time. Essentially, the Seek Journal challenges you to take what is often referred to as a "gratitude list" or a "good list" a step beyond basic bulleted items and to make meaning of those experiences through the lens of your relationship with God. Why were you grateful for this moment?

What might God be trying to tell you or what does this experience teach you about who God is? How might this knowledge help you concretely grow and live out your faith moving forward?

THE
SPIRITUAL
PRACTICE

What does the process look like?

In this fast paced world, hitting a pause button can be challenging for many of us, but the more that we learn to rest in prayer, the better we will become at recognizing how God is teaching us about Himself in our everyday lives. Though this process can look different for everyone, the format below will help you to rest in the moment and reflect on God's extraordinary love.

1. Take a few moments to slow down...take a few deep breaths... acknowledge the beautiful presence of God continually surrounding you.

2. Describe the ordinary moment that keeps coming up in your mind. Whether it happened today or occured months or even years ago, pause and reflect on it. No experience is too ordinary for God's love.

3. What initial emotions or feelings are surfacing? Name them.

4. Put yourself back in that moment and relive it bit by bit. Is there a specific part that sticks out to you the most?

5. Mentally place God in the moment and reflect on His role in the situation or setting. How is He participating? Be specific. What is He doing or saying? Is He taking the place of a person or is He a quiet observer?

6. What about God's participation changes your understanding of this experience? What does this ordinary moment teach you about God's love for you and the world? How might you go forward into the world with this knowledge?

7. End your time of reflection with a closing prayer: God, I thank you for the gift of extraordinary love in my ordinary life. Please help me to

continuously seek your heart and recognize the blessing of your presence all around me.

Each entry page of the Seek Journal will walk you through this exact reflection process, but if you find that you need additional guidance, you can flag this page and refer to the examples in the next section.

Throughout the Seek Journal, you'll also find beautiful scripture quotes that include the word seek. We prayerfully considered these verses and chose them with the hope that they will inspire you and help you as you reflect on God's extraordinary love.

SAMPLE REFLECTIONS AND TIPS

The following examples are based on real experiences and honest reflections.

You may choose to write out a narrative or you may prefer to use bullet points or even doodle or draw your responses. There is no right or wrong way to record your reflections. What is most important is to be open to the wondrous movement of God in your life.

MY ORDINARY MOMENT

Describe the moment as it happened.

*My daughter was tantruming over the fact that she couldn't
wear her favorite pink leggings. I tried over and over to
explain that they were in the laundry because she had worn
them two days in a row already and they had been caked over
with a layer of peanut butter and mud. She screamed at me
as I tried to keep my cool, remain patient, and continue with
my attempts to get us out the door on errands. Finally, she
came to me and asked for a hug. I got down on the floor and
wrapped my arms around her. She sobbed loudly into my chest.
I could feel her simultaneous anger toward me and her relief
at being in my arms. I hugged her and held her until she was
calm.*

What emotions are surfacing?
What about the experience do you feel called to ponder more deeply?

*Vulnerable, loved, remembering moments of frustration at how
my life was (or wasn't!) going.*

*Her loud sobs over my heart - the memory and the feeling of
that moment won't leave me.*

8 / 16 / 2018

GOD'S EXTRAORDINARY LOVE

Now place God in the moment with you.
What is His role in the scene?

Jesus is me in the story, and I am my daughter sobbing into His chest.

What is God trying to reveal to you about His love?

God loves me like I love my daughter...and even more so! I cling to him both when life goes well and when life doesn't go well. I tantrum and I cry. I laugh and I rejoice. I know this feeling of sobbing HARD into his Love, angry that MY plans for my life aren't happening. And yet, God pulls me closer. He allows me to remain in this place, in His peace, in His Love. It is in God's love that I find my grounding throughout life.

God, I thank you for the gift of extraordinary love in my ordinary life.
Please help me to continuously seek your heart and recognize the
blessing of your presence all around me.

AMEN.

MY ORDINARY MOMENT

Describe the moment as it happened.

Today, after lunch, I went into my room to fold a huge mountain of laundry on my bed. When I entered the room, I was stopped in my tracks by the sunlight pouring in from the window behind our master bed. It was streaming in brightly, dancing on the floor and bed comforter. I paused for a moment to watch the light form patterns and then fade out before I sat down. As I gazed out the window, I admired the leaves on our pecan trees as they swayed gently in the wind and the crisp blue of the Carolina sky.

What emotions are surfacing?
What about the experience do you feel called to ponder more deeply?

Though at first I felt rushed and frustrated, the longer I paused and reflected on the sight of nature in my own yard and bedroom, the more peace I felt. Though the moment was brief, it helped me to grow in gratitude and recenter my heart. I felt known and loved.

As I observed the light dancing merrily on the floor, I heard a quiet whisper in my heart - be still.

9 / 8 / 2018

GOD'S EXTRAORDINARY LOVE

Now place God in the moment with you.
What is His role in the scene?

*I feel like in this moment God was presenting himself to me
in the guise of the light. As the light stretched across the
floor, the Lord reached out to my heart, inviting me to be
still and cherish this moment with Him.*

What is God trying to reveal to you about His love?

*I tend to rush around so quickly that I forget to stop and
receive God's love. In this moment, I felt the Lord calling
me to pause, reflect, and cherish each moment. This moment
also reminded me to not get so caught up in the tiny
frustrations of day to day life, but to instead slow down and
savour the little things. There is beauty all around me - even
in something as simple and small as sunlight.*

God, I thank you for the gift of extraordinary love in my ordinary life.
Please help me to continuously seek your heart and recognize the
blessing of your presence all around me.

AMEN.

What other advice or tips will help me use the Seek Journal well?

Quieting our minds and our hearts is often the first challenge of prayer. Our world can be noisy and chaotic. It's okay if you struggle with silence; we do too. We've assembled a short list of suggestions to help you quiet down and settle into prayer at the back of this book (see page 236).

1. Reflecting and writing in the Seek Journal does not have to be done on any regular basis. Use the journal as often as you recognize a moment tugging on your heart that you believe to be calling you into deeper reflection. It may take you a few months or a year to fill the journal up. There is no set timeline.

2. Remember that no moment is too ordinary or boring or mundane for God's love. God is always with us. Always.

3. It is perfectly okay to record stories that sound similar or have similar lessons learned. Sometimes we need God to reveal a certain aspect of His love for us over and over again to bring us into an even deeper understanding of who He is or what plan He has for our lives.

4. After you've filled up the Seek Journal (and perhaps even before you've finished it), you might enjoy re-reading it and remembering various entries. Imagine looking through a diary or an album of mental snapshots of you and God. As you fill them out, the pages of this journal will contain a living history of how you have grown in your walk with Him, how He has healed your heart and molded your life. What a beautiful gift to reflect on! You also might find that revisiting certain entries will help you prepare for writing a reflection, discerning a difficult decision, or offering counsel to a friend.

Why is the Seek Journal integral to living today well?

Regardless of your season of life or vocation, living today well requires both rest and silence *and* movement and action. At times, God draws us away from the noisy, chaotic world to spend time with Him. He calls us to come away to the well, to be watered and nurtured by His divine love. He invites us to rest in Him during these moments of silence and quiet reflection.

But our God does not stop there. He also challenges us to share that glimpse of heaven with others and point those around us towards Him. He calls us to live out each day of our lives to its fullest, to let the work of our hands become a prayer rising to Him. He gives us the opportunity to glorify and bear witness to Him in the ordinary moments of our lives.

The spiritual practice of the Seek Journal helps you to live today well by both resting in the Lord's love and sharing that love with others. Each journaling question encourages you to reflect on the way God is working in your life and to move forward with courage and humility.

Whether moving forward means healing old wounds, cultivating gratitude, or shifting how you view the circumstances of your life, our hope is that this journal will help you to embrace both stillness and action in your day to day life.

THE
SEEK
JOURNAL

MY ORDINARY MOMENT

Describe the moment as it happened.

What emotions are surfacing?
What about the experience do you feel called to ponder more deeply?

_____/_____/_____

GOD'S EXTRAORDINARY LOVE

Now place God in the moment with you.
What is His role in the scene?

What is God trying to reveal to you about His love?

God, I thank you for the gift of extraordinary love in my ordinary life.
Please help me to continuously seek your heart and recognize the
blessing of your presence all around me.

AMEN.

MY ORDINARY MOMENT

Describe the moment as it happened.

What emotions are surfacing?
What about the experience do you feel called to ponder more deeply?

_____ / _____ / _____

GOD'S EXTRAORDINARY LOVE

Now place God in the moment with you.
What is His role in the scene?

What is God trying to reveal to you about His love?

God, I thank you for the gift of extraordinary love in my ordinary life.
Please help me to continuously seek your heart and recognize the
blessing of your presence all around me.

AMEN.

MY ORDINARY MOMENT

Describe the moment as it happened.

What emotions are surfacing?
What about the experience do you feel called to ponder more deeply?

_____/_____/_____

Now place God in the moment with you.
What is His role in the scene?

What is God trying to reveal to you about His love?

God, I thank you for the gift of extraordinary love in my ordinary life.
Please help me to continuously seek your heart and recognize the
blessing of your presence all around me.

AMEN.

MY ORDINARY MOMENT

Describe the moment as it happened.

What emotions are surfacing?
What about the experience do you feel called to ponder more deeply?

_____ / _____ / _____

GOD'S EXTRAORDINARY LOVE

Now place God in the moment with you.
What is His role in the scene?

What is God trying to reveal to you about His love?

God, I thank you for the gift of extraordinary love in my ordinary life.
Please help me to continuously seek your heart and recognize the
blessing of your presence all around me.

AMEN.

MY ORDINARY MOMENT

Describe the moment as it happened.

What emotions are surfacing?
What about the experience do you feel called to ponder more deeply?

_____ / _____ / _____

GOD'S EXTRAORDINARY LOVE

Now place God in the moment with you.
What is His role in the scene?

What is God trying to reveal to you about His love?

God, I thank you for the gift of extraordinary love in my ordinary life.
Please help me to continuously seek your heart and recognize the
blessing of your presence all around me.

AMEN.

MY ORDINARY MOMENT

Describe the moment as it happened.

What emotions are surfacing?
What about the experience do you feel called to ponder more deeply?

___/___/___

GOD'S EXTRAORDINARY LOVE

Now place God in the moment with you.
What is His role in the scene?

What is God trying to reveal to you about His love?

God, I thank you for the gift of extraordinary love in my ordinary life.
Please help me to continuously seek your heart and recognize the
blessing of your presence all around me.

AMEN.

MY ORDINARY MOMENT

Describe the moment as it happened.

What emotions are surfacing?
What about the experience do you feel called to ponder more deeply?

_____/_____/_____

GOD'S EXTRAORDINARY LOVE

Now place God in the moment with you.
What is His role in the scene?

What is God trying to reveal to you about His love?

God, I thank you for the gift of extraordinary love in my ordinary life.
Please help me to continuously seek your heart and recognize the
blessing of your presence all around me.

AMEN.

MY ORDINARY MOMENT

Describe the moment as it happened.

What emotions are surfacing?
What about the experience do you feel called to ponder more deeply?

___/___/___

GOD'S EXTRAORDINARY LOVE

Now place God in the moment with you.
What is His role in the scene?

What is God trying to reveal to you about His love?

God, I thank you for the gift of extraordinary love in my ordinary life.
Please help me to continuously seek your heart and recognize the
blessing of your presence all around me.

AMEN.

MY ORDINARY MOMENT

Describe the moment as it happened.

What emotions are surfacing?
What about the experience do you feel called to ponder more deeply?

_____/_____/_____

GOD'S EXTRAORDINARY LOVE

Now place God in the moment with you.
What is His role in the scene?

What is God trying to reveal to you about His love?

God, I thank you for the gift of extraordinary love in my ordinary life.
Please help me to continuously seek your heart and recognize the
blessing of your presence all around me.

AMEN.

MY ORDINARY MOMENT

Describe the moment as it happened.

What emotions are surfacing?
What about the experience do you feel called to ponder more deeply?

_____ / _____ / _____

GOD'S EXTRAORDINARY LOVE

Now place God in the moment with you.
What is His role in the scene?

What is God trying to reveal to you about His love?

God, I thank you for the gift of extraordinary love in my ordinary life.
Please help me to continuously seek your heart and recognize the
blessing of your presence all around me.

AMEN.

MY ORDINARY MOMENT

Describe the moment as it happened.

What emotions are surfacing?
What about the experience do you feel called to ponder more deeply?

_____/_____/_____

GOD'S EXTRAORDINARY LOVE

Now place God in the moment with you.
What is His role in the scene?

What is God trying to reveal to you about His love?

God, I thank you for the gift of extraordinary love in my ordinary life.
Please help me to continuously seek your heart and recognize the
blessing of your presence all around me.

AMEN.

MY ORDINARY MOMENT

Describe the moment as it happened.

What emotions are surfacing?
What about the experience do you feel called to ponder more deeply?

_____ / _____ / _____

Now place God in the moment with you.
What is His role in the scene?

What is God trying to reveal to you about His love?

God, I thank you for the gift of extraordinary love in my ordinary life.
Please help me to continuously seek your heart and recognize the
blessing of your presence all around me.

AMEN.

MY ORDINARY MOMENT

Describe the moment as it happened.

What emotions are surfacing?
What about the experience do you feel called to ponder more deeply?

_____/_____/_____

GOD'S EXTRAORDINARY LOVE

Now place God in the moment with you.
What is His role in the scene?

What is God trying to reveal to you about His love?

God, I thank you for the gift of extraordinary love in my ordinary life.
Please help me to continuously seek your heart and recognize the
blessing of your presence all around me.

AMEN.

MY ORDINARY MOMENT

Describe the moment as it happened.

What emotions are surfacing?
What about the experience do you feel called to ponder more deeply?

___/___/___

GOD'S EXTRAORDINARY LOVE

Now place God in the moment with you.
What is His role in the scene?

What is God trying to reveal to you about His love?

God, I thank you for the gift of extraordinary love in my ordinary life.
Please help me to continuously seek your heart and recognize the
blessing of your presence all around me.

AMEN.

MY ORDINARY MOMENT

Describe the moment as it happened.

What emotions are surfacing?
What about the experience do you feel called to ponder more deeply?

_____ / _____ / _____

GOD'S EXTRAORDINARY LOVE

Now place God in the moment with you.
What is His role in the scene?

What is God trying to reveal to you about His love?

God, I thank you for the gift of extraordinary love in my ordinary life.
Please help me to continuously seek your heart and recognize the
blessing of your presence all around me.

AMEN.

MY ORDINARY MOMENT

Describe the moment as it happened.

What emotions are surfacing?
What about the experience do you feel called to ponder more deeply?

_____ / _____ / _____

Now place God in the moment with you.
What is His role in the scene?

What is God trying to reveal to you about His love?

God, I thank you for the gift of extraordinary love in my ordinary life.
Please help me to continuously seek your heart and recognize the
blessing of your presence all around me.

AMEN.

MY ORDINARY MOMENT

Describe the moment as it happened.

What emotions are surfacing?
What about the experience do you feel called to ponder more deeply?

_____/_____/_____

GOD'S EXTRAORDINARY LOVE

Now place God in the moment with you.
What is His role in the scene?

What is God trying to reveal to you about His love?

God, I thank you for the gift of extraordinary love in my ordinary life.
Please help me to continuously seek your heart and recognize the
blessing of your presence all around me.

AMEN.

MY ORDINARY MOMENT

Describe the moment as it happened.

What emotions are surfacing?
What about the experience do you feel called to ponder more deeply?

_____/_____/_____

GOD'S EXTRAORDINARY LOVE

Now place God in the moment with you.
What is His role in the scene?

What is God trying to reveal to you about His love?

God, I thank you for the gift of extraordinary love in my ordinary life.
Please help me to continuously seek your heart and recognize the
blessing of your presence all around me.

AMEN.

MY ORDINARY MOMENT

Describe the moment as it happened.

What emotions are surfacing?
What about the experience do you feel called to ponder more deeply?

_____/_____/_____

GOD'S EXTRAORDINARY LOVE

Now place God in the moment with you.
What is His role in the scene?

What is God trying to reveal to you about His love?

God, I thank you for the gift of extraordinary love in my ordinary life.
Please help me to continuously seek your heart and recognize the
blessing of your presence all around me.

AMEN.

MY ORDINARY MOMENT

Describe the moment as it happened.

What emotions are surfacing?
What about the experience do you feel called to ponder more deeply?

_____ / _____ / _____

GOD'S EXTRAORDINARY LOVE

Now place God in the moment with you.
What is His role in the scene?

What is God trying to reveal to you about His love?

God, I thank you for the gift of extraordinary love in my ordinary life.
Please help me to continuously seek your heart and recognize the
blessing of your presence all around me.

AMEN.

Seek
the Lord
and
His strength,

seek His
presence
continually.

1 Chronicles 16:11

MY ORDINARY MOMENT

Describe the moment as it happened.

What emotions are surfacing?
What about the experience do you feel called to ponder more deeply?

_____/_____/_____

GOD'S EXTRAORDINARY LOVE

Now place God in the moment with you.
What is His role in the scene?

What is God trying to reveal to you about His love?

God, I thank you for the gift of extraordinary love in my ordinary life.
Please help me to continuously seek your heart and recognize the
blessing of your presence all around me.

AMEN.

MY ORDINARY MOMENT

Describe the moment as it happened.

What emotions are surfacing?
What about the experience do you feel called to ponder more deeply?

_____ / _____ / _____

GOD'S EXTRAORDINARY LOVE

Now place God in the moment with you.
What is His role in the scene?

What is God trying to reveal to you about His love?

God, I thank you for the gift of extraordinary love in my ordinary life.
Please help me to continuously seek your heart and recognize the
blessing of your presence all around me.

AMEN.

MY ORDINARY MOMENT

Describe the moment as it happened.

What emotions are surfacing?
What about the experience do you feel called to ponder more deeply?

_____ / _____ / _____

GOD'S EXTRAORDINARY LOVE

Now place God in the moment with you.
What is His role in the scene?

What is God trying to reveal to you about His love?

God, I thank you for the gift of extraordinary love in my ordinary life.
Please help me to continuously seek your heart and recognize the
blessing of your presence all around me.

AMEN.

MY ORDINARY MOMENT

Describe the moment as it happened.

What emotions are surfacing?
What about the experience do you feel called to ponder more deeply?

/   /

GOD'S EXTRAORDINARY LOVE

Now place God in the moment with you.
What is His role in the scene?

What is God trying to reveal to you about His love?

God, I thank you for the gift of extraordinary love in my ordinary life.
Please help me to continuously seek your heart and recognize the
blessing of your presence all around me.

AMEN.

MY ORDINARY MOMENT

Describe the moment as it happened.

What emotions are surfacing?
What about the experience do you feel called to ponder more deeply?

_____ / _____ / _____

GOD'S EXTRAORDINARY LOVE

Now place God in the moment with you.
What is His role in the scene?

What is God trying to reveal to you about His love?

God, I thank you for the gift of extraordinary love in my ordinary life.
Please help me to continuously seek your heart and recognize the
blessing of your presence all around me.

AMEN.

MY ORDINARY MOMENT

Describe the moment as it happened.

What emotions are surfacing?
What about the experience do you feel called to ponder more deeply?

_____ / _____ / _____

GOD'S EXTRAORDINARY LOVE

Now place God in the moment with you.
What is His role in the scene?

What is God trying to reveal to you about His love?

God, I thank you for the gift of extraordinary love in my ordinary life.
Please help me to continuously seek your heart and recognize the
blessing of your presence all around me.

AMEN.

MY ORDINARY MOMENT

Describe the moment as it happened.

What emotions are surfacing?
What about the experience do you feel called to ponder more deeply?

_____ / ____ / _____

GOD'S EXTRAORDINARY LOVE

Now place God in the moment with you.
What is His role in the scene?

What is God trying to reveal to you about His love?

God, I thank you for the gift of extraordinary love in my ordinary life.
Please help me to continuously seek your heart and recognize the
blessing of your presence all around me.

AMEN.

MY ORDINARY MOMENT

Describe the moment as it happened.

What emotions are surfacing?
What about the experience do you feel called to ponder more deeply?

_____ / _____ / _____

GOD'S EXTRAORDINARY LOVE

Now place God in the moment with you.
What is His role in the scene?

What is God trying to reveal to you about His love?

God, I thank you for the gift of extraordinary love in my ordinary life.
Please help me to continuously seek your heart and recognize the
blessing of your presence all around me.

AMEN.

MY ORDINARY MOMENT

Describe the moment as it happened.

What emotions are surfacing?
What about the experience do you feel called to ponder more deeply?

/   /

Now place God in the moment with you.
What is His role in the scene?

What is God trying to reveal to you about His love?

God, I thank you for the gift of extraordinary love in my ordinary life.
Please help me to continuously seek your heart and recognize the
blessing of your presence all around me.

AMEN.

MY ORDINARY MOMENT

Describe the moment as it happened.

What emotions are surfacing?
What about the experience do you feel called to ponder more deeply?

_____ / _____ / _____

GOD'S EXTRAORDINARY LOVE

Now place God in the moment with you.
What is His role in the scene?

What is God trying to reveal to you about His love?

God, I thank you for the gift of extraordinary love in my ordinary life.
Please help me to continuously seek your heart and recognize the
blessing of your presence all around me.

AMEN.

MY ORDINARY MOMENT

Describe the moment as it happened.

What emotions are surfacing?
What about the experience do you feel called to ponder more deeply?

_____/_____/_____

GOD'S EXTRAORDINARY LOVE

Now place God in the moment with you.
What is His role in the scene?

What is God trying to reveal to you about His love?

God, I thank you for the gift of extraordinary love in my ordinary life.
Please help me to continuously seek your heart and recognize the
blessing of your presence all around me.

AMEN.

MY ORDINARY MOMENT

Describe the moment as it happened.

What emotions are surfacing?
What about the experience do you feel called to ponder more deeply?

_____/_____/_____

GOD'S EXTRAORDINARY LOVE

Now place God in the moment with you.
What is His role in the scene?

What is God trying to reveal to you about His love?

God, I thank you for the gift of extraordinary love in my ordinary life.
Please help me to continuously seek your heart and recognize the
blessing of your presence all around me.

AMEN.

MY ORDINARY MOMENT

Describe the moment as it happened.

What emotions are surfacing?
What about the experience do you feel called to ponder more deeply?

_____ / _____ / _____

GOD'S EXTRAORDINARY LOVE

Now place God in the moment with you.
What is His role in the scene?

What is God trying to reveal to you about His love?

God, I thank you for the gift of extraordinary love in my ordinary life.
Please help me to continuously seek your heart and recognize the
blessing of your presence all around me.

AMEN.

MY ORDINARY MOMENT

Describe the moment as it happened.

What emotions are surfacing?
What about the experience do you feel called to ponder more deeply?

_____ / _____ / _____

GOD'S EXTRAORDINARY LOVE

Now place God in the moment with you.
What is His role in the scene?

What is God trying to reveal to you about His love?

God, I thank you for the gift of extraordinary love in my ordinary life.
Please help me to continuously seek your heart and recognize the
blessing of your presence all around me.

AMEN.

MY ORDINARY MOMENT

Describe the moment as it happened.

What emotions are surfacing?
What about the experience do you feel called to ponder more deeply?

_____ / _____ / _____

GOD'S EXTRAORDINARY LOVE

Now place God in the moment with you.
What is His role in the scene?

What is God trying to reveal to you about His love?

God, I thank you for the gift of extraordinary love in my ordinary life.
Please help me to continuously seek your heart and recognize the
blessing of your presence all around me.

AMEN.

MY ORDINARY MOMENT

Describe the moment as it happened.

What emotions are surfacing?
What about the experience do you feel called to ponder more deeply?

_____ / _____ / _____

Now place God in the moment with you.
What is His role in the scene?

What is God trying to reveal to you about His love?

God, I thank you for the gift of extraordinary love in my ordinary life.
Please help me to continuously seek your heart and recognize the
blessing of your presence all around me.

AMEN.

MY ORDINARY MOMENT

Describe the moment as it happened.

What emotions are surfacing?
What about the experience do you feel called to ponder more deeply?

_____ / _____ / _____

Now place God in the moment with you.
What is His role in the scene?

What is God trying to reveal to you about His love?

God, I thank you for the gift of extraordinary love in my ordinary life.
Please help me to continuously seek your heart and recognize the
blessing of your presence all around me.

AMEN.

MY ORDINARY MOMENT

Describe the moment as it happened.

What emotions are surfacing?
What about the experience do you feel called to ponder more deeply?

_____ / _____ / _____

Now place God in the moment with you.
What is His role in the scene?

What is God trying to reveal to you about His love?

God, I thank you for the gift of extraordinary love in my ordinary life.
Please help me to continuously seek your heart and recognize the
blessing of your presence all around me.

AMEN.

MY ORDINARY MOMENT

Describe the moment as it happened.

What emotions are surfacing?
What about the experience do you feel called to ponder more deeply?

_____ / _____ / _____

Now place God in the moment with you.
What is His role in the scene?

What is God trying to reveal to you about His love?

God, I thank you for the gift of extraordinary love in my ordinary life.
Please help me to continuously seek your heart and recognize the
blessing of your presence all around me.

AMEN.

MY ORDINARY MOMENT

Describe the moment as it happened.

What emotions are surfacing?
What about the experience do you feel called to ponder more deeply?

_____ / _____ / _____

GOD'S EXTRAORDINARY LOVE

Now place God in the moment with you.
What is His role in the scene?

What is God trying to reveal to you about His love?

God, I thank you for the gift of extraordinary love in my ordinary life.
Please help me to continuously seek your heart and recognize the
blessing of your presence all around me.

AMEN.

O God,
you are
my God,
I seek you,

my soul
thirsts
for
you.

Psalm 63:1

MY ORDINARY MOMENT

Describe the moment as it happened.

What emotions are surfacing?
What about the experience do you feel called to ponder more deeply?

_____ / _____ / _____

GOD'S EXTRAORDINARY LOVE

Now place God in the moment with you.
What is His role in the scene?

What is God trying to reveal to you about His love?

God, I thank you for the gift of extraordinary love in my ordinary life.
Please help me to continuously seek your heart and recognize the
blessing of your presence all around me.

AMEN.

MY ORDINARY MOMENT

Describe the moment as it happened.

What emotions are surfacing?
What about the experience do you feel called to ponder more deeply?

_____/_____/_____

Now place God in the moment with you.
What is His role in the scene?

What is God trying to reveal to you about His love?

God, I thank you for the gift of extraordinary love in my ordinary life.
Please help me to continuously seek your heart and recognize the
blessing of your presence all around me.

AMEN.

MY ORDINARY MOMENT

Describe the moment as it happened.

What emotions are surfacing?
What about the experience do you feel called to ponder more deeply?

_____ / _____ / _____

GOD'S EXTRAORDINARY LOVE

Now place God in the moment with you.
What is His role in the scene?

What is God trying to reveal to you about His love?

God, I thank you for the gift of extraordinary love in my ordinary life.
Please help me to continuously seek your heart and recognize the
blessing of your presence all around me.

AMEN.

MY ORDINARY MOMENT

Describe the moment as it happened.

What emotions are surfacing?
What about the experience do you feel called to ponder more deeply?

_____ / _____ / _____

GOD'S EXTRAORDINARY LOVE

Now place God in the moment with you.
What is His role in the scene?

What is God trying to reveal to you about His love?

God, I thank you for the gift of extraordinary love in my ordinary life.
Please help me to continuously seek your heart and recognize the
blessing of your presence all around me.

AMEN.

MY ORDINARY MOMENT

Describe the moment as it happened.

What emotions are surfacing?
What about the experience do you feel called to ponder more deeply?

_____/_____/_____

GOD'S EXTRAORDINARY LOVE

Now place God in the moment with you.
What is His role in the scene?

What is God trying to reveal to you about His love?

God, I thank you for the gift of extraordinary love in my ordinary life.
Please help me to continuously seek your heart and recognize the
blessing of your presence all around me.

AMEN.

MY ORDINARY MOMENT

Describe the moment as it happened.

What emotions are surfacing?
What about the experience do you feel called to ponder more deeply?

_____/_____/_____

GOD'S EXTRAORDINARY LOVE

Now place God in the moment with you.
What is His role in the scene?

What is God trying to reveal to you about His love?

God, I thank you for the gift of extraordinary love in my ordinary life.
Please help me to continuously seek your heart and recognize the
blessing of your presence all around me.

AMEN.

MY ORDINARY MOMENT

Describe the moment as it happened.

What emotions are surfacing?
What about the experience do you feel called to ponder more deeply?

_____/_____/_____

GOD'S EXTRAORDINARY LOVE

Now place God in the moment with you.
What is His role in the scene?

What is God trying to reveal to you about His love?

God, I thank you for the gift of extraordinary love in my ordinary life.
Please help me to continuously seek your heart and recognize the
blessing of your presence all around me.

AMEN.

MY ORDINARY MOMENT

Describe the moment as it happened.

What emotions are surfacing?
What about the experience do you feel called to ponder more deeply?

_____/_____/_____

GOD'S EXTRAORDINARY LOVE

Now place God in the moment with you.
What is His role in the scene?

What is God trying to reveal to you about His love?

God, I thank you for the gift of extraordinary love in my ordinary life.
Please help me to continuously seek your heart and recognize the
blessing of your presence all around me.

AMEN.

MY ORDINARY MOMENT

Describe the moment as it happened.

What emotions are surfacing?
What about the experience do you feel called to ponder more deeply?

_____ / _____ / _____

GOD'S EXTRAORDINARY LOVE

Now place God in the moment with you.
What is His role in the scene?

What is God trying to reveal to you about His love?

God, I thank you for the gift of extraordinary love in my ordinary life.
Please help me to continuously seek your heart and recognize the
blessing of your presence all around me.

AMEN.

MY ORDINARY MOMENT

Describe the moment as it happened.

What emotions are surfacing?
What about the experience do you feel called to ponder more deeply?

_____ / _____ / _____

GOD'S EXTRAORDINARY LOVE

Now place God in the moment with you.
What is His role in the scene?

What is God trying to reveal to you about His love?

God, I thank you for the gift of extraordinary love in my ordinary life.
Please help me to continuously seek your heart and recognize the
blessing of your presence all around me.

AMEN.

MY ORDINARY MOMENT

Describe the moment as it happened.

What emotions are surfacing?
What about the experience do you feel called to ponder more deeply?

_____/_____/_____

GOD'S EXTRAORDINARY LOVE

Now place God in the moment with you.
What is His role in the scene?

What is God trying to reveal to you about His love?

God, I thank you for the gift of extraordinary love in my ordinary life.
Please help me to continuously seek your heart and recognize the
blessing of your presence all around me.

AMEN.

MY ORDINARY MOMENT

Describe the moment as it happened.

What emotions are surfacing?
What about the experience do you feel called to ponder more deeply?

_____ / _____ / _____

GOD'S EXTRAORDINARY LOVE

Now place God in the moment with you.
What is His role in the scene?

What is God trying to reveal to you about His love?

God, I thank you for the gift of extraordinary love in my ordinary life.
Please help me to continuously seek your heart and recognize the
blessing of your presence all around me.

AMEN.

MY ORDINARY MOMENT

Describe the moment as it happened.

What emotions are surfacing?
What about the experience do you feel called to ponder more deeply?

_____ / _____ / _____

GOD'S EXTRAORDINARY LOVE

Now place God in the moment with you.
What is His role in the scene?

What is God trying to reveal to you about His love?

God, I thank you for the gift of extraordinary love in my ordinary life.
Please help me to continuously seek your heart and recognize the
blessing of your presence all around me.

AMEN.

MY ORDINARY MOMENT

Describe the moment as it happened.

What emotions are surfacing?
What about the experience do you feel called to ponder more deeply?

_____ / _____ / _____

GOD'S EXTRAORDINARY LOVE

Now place God in the moment with you.
What is His role in the scene?

What is God trying to reveal to you about His love?

God, I thank you for the gift of extraordinary love in my ordinary life.
Please help me to continuously seek your heart and recognize the
blessing of your presence all around me.

AMEN.

MY ORDINARY MOMENT

Describe the moment as it happened.

What emotions are surfacing?
What about the experience do you feel called to ponder more deeply?

_____ / _____ / _____

GOD'S EXTRAORDINARY LOVE

Now place God in the moment with you.
What is His role in the scene?

What is God trying to reveal to you about His love?

God, I thank you for the gift of extraordinary love in my ordinary life.
Please help me to continuously seek your heart and recognize the
blessing of your presence all around me.

AMEN.

MY ORDINARY MOMENT

Describe the moment as it happened.

What emotions are surfacing?
What about the experience do you feel called to ponder more deeply?

_____ / _____ / _____

GOD'S EXTRAORDINARY LOVE

Now place God in the moment with you.
What is His role in the scene?

What is God trying to reveal to you about His love?

God, I thank you for the gift of extraordinary love in my ordinary life.
Please help me to continuously seek your heart and recognize the
blessing of your presence all around me.

AMEN.

MY ORDINARY MOMENT

Describe the moment as it happened.

What emotions are surfacing?
What about the experience do you feel called to ponder more deeply?

_____/_____/_____

GOD'S EXTRAORDINARY LOVE

Now place God in the moment with you.
What is His role in the scene?

What is God trying to reveal to you about His love?

God, I thank you for the gift of extraordinary love in my ordinary life.
Please help me to continuously seek your heart and recognize the
blessing of your presence all around me.

AMEN.

MY ORDINARY MOMENT

Describe the moment as it happened.

What emotions are surfacing?
What about the experience do you feel called to ponder more deeply?

_____ / _____ / _____

Now place God in the moment with you.
What is His role in the scene?

What is God trying to reveal to you about His love?

God, I thank you for the gift of extraordinary love in my ordinary life.
Please help me to continuously seek your heart and recognize the
blessing of your presence all around me.

AMEN.

MY ORDINARY MOMENT

Describe the moment as it happened.

What emotions are surfacing?
What about the experience do you feel called to ponder more deeply?

____/____/____

GOD'S EXTRAORDINARY LOVE

Now place God in the moment with you.
What is His role in the scene?

What is God trying to reveal to you about His love?

God, I thank you for the gift of extraordinary love in my ordinary life.
Please help me to continuously seek your heart and recognize the
blessing of your presence all around me.

AMEN.

MY ORDINARY MOMENT

Describe the moment as it happened.

What emotions are surfacing?
What about the experience do you feel called to ponder more deeply?

/   /

GOD'S EXTRAORDINARY LOVE

Now place God in the moment with you.
What is His role in the scene?

What is God trying to reveal to you about His love?

God, I thank you for the gift of extraordinary love in my ordinary life.
Please help me to continuously seek your heart and recognize the
blessing of your presence all around me.

AMEN.

When you search for me
you will find me;
if you seek me with all your heart,

I will let you
find me, says the Lord.

Jeremiah 29:13

MY ORDINARY MOMENT

Describe the moment as it happened.

What emotions are surfacing?
What about the experience do you feel called to ponder more deeply?

_____ / _____ / _____

GOD'S EXTRAORDINARY LOVE

Now place God in the moment with you.
What is His role in the scene?

What is God trying to reveal to you about His love?

God, I thank you for the gift of extraordinary love in my ordinary life.
Please help me to continuously seek your heart and recognize the
blessing of your presence all around me.

AMEN.

MY ORDINARY MOMENT

Describe the moment as it happened.

What emotions are surfacing?
What about the experience do you feel called to ponder more deeply?

_____ / _____ / _____

GOD'S EXTRAORDINARY LOVE

Now place God in the moment with you.
What is His role in the scene?

What is God trying to reveal to you about His love?

God, I thank you for the gift of extraordinary love in my ordinary life.
Please help me to continuously seek your heart and recognize the
blessing of your presence all around me.

AMEN.

MY ORDINARY MOMENT

Describe the moment as it happened.

What emotions are surfacing?
What about the experience do you feel called to ponder more deeply?

/   /

GOD'S EXTRAORDINARY LOVE

Now place God in the moment with you.
What is His role in the scene?

What is God trying to reveal to you about His love?

God, I thank you for the gift of extraordinary love in my ordinary life.
Please help me to continuously seek your heart and recognize the
blessing of your presence all around me.

AMEN.

MY ORDINARY MOMENT

Describe the moment as it happened.

What emotions are surfacing?
What about the experience do you feel called to ponder more deeply?

_____/_____/_____

GOD'S EXTRAORDINARY LOVE

Now place God in the moment with you.
What is His role in the scene?

What is God trying to reveal to you about His love?

God, I thank you for the gift of extraordinary love in my ordinary life.
Please help me to continuously seek your heart and recognize the
blessing of your presence all around me.

AMEN.

MY ORDINARY MOMENT

Describe the moment as it happened.

What emotions are surfacing?
What about the experience do you feel called to ponder more deeply?

_____/_____/_____

GOD'S EXTRAORDINARY LOVE

Now place God in the moment with you.
What is His role in the scene?

What is God trying to reveal to you about His love?

God, I thank you for the gift of extraordinary love in my ordinary life.
Please help me to continuously seek your heart and recognize the
blessing of your presence all around me.

AMEN.

MY ORDINARY MOMENT

Describe the moment as it happened.

What emotions are surfacing?
What about the experience do you feel called to ponder more deeply?

_____ / _____ / _____

GOD'S EXTRAORDINARY LOVE

Now place God in the moment with you.
What is His role in the scene?

What is God trying to reveal to you about His love?

God, I thank you for the gift of extraordinary love in my ordinary life.
Please help me to continuously seek your heart and recognize the
blessing of your presence all around me.

AMEN.

MY ORDINARY MOMENT

Describe the moment as it happened.

What emotions are surfacing?
What about the experience do you feel called to ponder more deeply?

_____ / _____ / _____

GOD'S EXTRAORDINARY LOVE

Now place God in the moment with you.
What is His role in the scene?

What is God trying to reveal to you about His love?

God, I thank you for the gift of extraordinary love in my ordinary life.
Please help me to continuously seek your heart and recognize the
blessing of your presence all around me.

AMEN.

MY ORDINARY MOMENT

Describe the moment as it happened.

What emotions are surfacing?
What about the experience do you feel called to ponder more deeply?

_____/_____/_____

GOD'S EXTRAORDINARY LOVE

Now place God in the moment with you.
What is His role in the scene?

What is God trying to reveal to you about His love?

God, I thank you for the gift of extraordinary love in my ordinary life.
Please help me to continuously seek your heart and recognize the
blessing of your presence all around me.

AMEN.

MY ORDINARY MOMENT

Describe the moment as it happened.

What emotions are surfacing?
What about the experience do you feel called to ponder more deeply?

_____ / _____ / _____

GOD'S EXTRAORDINARY LOVE

Now place God in the moment with you.
What is His role in the scene?

What is God trying to reveal to you about His love?

God, I thank you for the gift of extraordinary love in my ordinary life.
Please help me to continuously seek your heart and recognize the
blessing of your presence all around me.

AMEN.

MY ORDINARY MOMENT

Describe the moment as it happened.

What emotions are surfacing?
What about the experience do you feel called to ponder more deeply?

_____ / _____ / _____

GOD'S EXTRAORDINARY LOVE

Now place God in the moment with you.
What is His role in the scene?

What is God trying to reveal to you about His love?

God, I thank you for the gift of extraordinary love in my ordinary life.
Please help me to continuously seek your heart and recognize the
blessing of your presence all around me.

AMEN.

MY ORDINARY MOMENT

Describe the moment as it happened.

What emotions are surfacing?
What about the experience do you feel called to ponder more deeply?

_____ / _____ / _____

GOD'S EXTRAORDINARY LOVE

Now place God in the moment with you.
What is His role in the scene?

What is God trying to reveal to you about His love?

God, I thank you for the gift of extraordinary love in my ordinary life.
Please help me to continuously seek your heart and recognize the
blessing of your presence all around me.

AMEN.

MY ORDINARY MOMENT

Describe the moment as it happened.

What emotions are surfacing?
What about the experience do you feel called to ponder more deeply?

_____/_____/_____

GOD'S EXTRAORDINARY LOVE

Now place God in the moment with you.
What is His role in the scene?

What is God trying to reveal to you about His love?

God, I thank you for the gift of extraordinary love in my ordinary life.
Please help me to continuously seek your heart and recognize the
blessing of your presence all around me.

AMEN.

MY ORDINARY MOMENT

Describe the moment as it happened.

What emotions are surfacing?
What about the experience do you feel called to ponder more deeply?

_____ / _____ / _____

GOD'S EXTRAORDINARY LOVE

Now place God in the moment with you.
What is His role in the scene?

What is God trying to reveal to you about His love?

God, I thank you for the gift of extraordinary love in my ordinary life.
Please help me to continuously seek your heart and recognize the
blessing of your presence all around me.

AMEN.

MY ORDINARY MOMENT

Describe the moment as it happened.

What emotions are surfacing?
What about the experience do you feel called to ponder more deeply?

_____ / _____ / _____

GOD'S EXTRAORDINARY LOVE

Now place God in the moment with you.
What is His role in the scene?

What is God trying to reveal to you about His love?

God, I thank you for the gift of extraordinary love in my ordinary life.
Please help me to continuously seek your heart and recognize the
blessing of your presence all around me.

AMEN.

MY ORDINARY MOMENT

Describe the moment as it happened.

What emotions are surfacing?
What about the experience do you feel called to ponder more deeply?

_____/_____/_____

GOD'S EXTRAORDINARY LOVE

Now place God in the moment with you.
What is His role in the scene?

What is God trying to reveal to you about His love?

God, I thank you for the gift of extraordinary love in my ordinary life.
Please help me to continuously seek your heart and recognize the
blessing of your presence all around me.

AMEN.

MY ORDINARY MOMENT

Describe the moment as it happened.

What emotions are surfacing?
What about the experience do you feel called to ponder more deeply?

_____/_____/_____

GOD'S EXTRAORDINARY LOVE

Now place God in the moment with you.
What is His role in the scene?

What is God trying to reveal to you about His love?

God, I thank you for the gift of extraordinary love in my ordinary life.
Please help me to continuously seek your heart and recognize the
blessing of your presence all around me.

AMEN.

MY ORDINARY MOMENT

Describe the moment as it happened.

What emotions are surfacing?
What about the experience do you feel called to ponder more deeply?

/   /

GOD'S EXTRAORDINARY LOVE

Now place God in the moment with you.
What is His role in the scene?

What is God trying to reveal to you about His love?

God, I thank you for the gift of extraordinary love in my ordinary life.
Please help me to continuously seek your heart and recognize the
blessing of your presence all around me.

AMEN.

MY ORDINARY MOMENT

Describe the moment as it happened.

What emotions are surfacing?
What about the experience do you feel called to ponder more deeply?

_____ / _____ / _____

GOD'S EXTRAORDINARY LOVE

Now place God in the moment with you.
What is His role in the scene?

What is God trying to reveal to you about His love?

God, I thank you for the gift of extraordinary love in my ordinary life.
Please help me to continuously seek your heart and recognize the
blessing of your presence all around me.

AMEN.

MY ORDINARY MOMENT

Describe the moment as it happened.

What emotions are surfacing?
What about the experience do you feel called to ponder more deeply?

_____/_____/_____

GOD'S EXTRAORDINARY LOVE

Now place God in the moment with you.
What is His role in the scene?

What is God trying to reveal to you about His love?

God, I thank you for the gift of extraordinary love in my ordinary life.
Please help me to continuously seek your heart and recognize the
blessing of your presence all around me.

AMEN.

MY ORDINARY MOMENT

Describe the moment as it happened.

What emotions are surfacing?
What about the experience do you feel called to ponder more deeply?

___/___/___

GOD'S EXTRAORDINARY LOVE

Now place God in the moment with you.
What is His role in the scene?

What is God trying to reveal to you about His love?

God, I thank you for the gift of extraordinary love in my ordinary life.
Please help me to continuously seek your heart and recognize the
blessing of your presence all around me.

AMEN.

One thing
I asked
of the Lord,
that I will
seek after:
to live
in the house
of the Lord
all the days
of my life,
to behold
the beauty
of the Lord
and to inquire
in his temple.

Psalm 27:4

MY ORDINARY MOMENT

Describe the moment as it happened.

What emotions are surfacing?
What about the experience do you feel called to ponder more deeply?

_____/_____/_____

GOD'S EXTRAORDINARY LOVE

Now place God in the moment with you.
What is His role in the scene?

What is God trying to reveal to you about His love?

God, I thank you for the gift of extraordinary love in my ordinary life.
Please help me to continuously seek your heart and recognize the
blessing of your presence all around me.

AMEN.

MY ORDINARY MOMENT

Describe the moment as it happened.

What emotions are surfacing?
What about the experience do you feel called to ponder more deeply?

_____/_____/_____

GOD'S EXTRAORDINARY LOVE

Now place God in the moment with you.
What is His role in the scene?

What is God trying to reveal to you about His love?

God, I thank you for the gift of extraordinary love in my ordinary life.
Please help me to continuously seek your heart and recognize the
blessing of your presence all around me.

AMEN.

Describe the moment as it happened.

What emotions are surfacing?
What about the experience do you feel called to ponder more deeply?

_____ / _____ / _____

GOD'S EXTRAORDINARY LOVE

Now place God in the moment with you.
What is His role in the scene?

What is God trying to reveal to you about His love?

God, I thank you for the gift of extraordinary love in my ordinary life.
Please help me to continuously seek your heart and recognize the
blessing of your presence all around me.

AMEN.

MY ORDINARY MOMENT

Describe the moment as it happened.

What emotions are surfacing?
What about the experience do you feel called to ponder more deeply?

_____/_____/_____

GOD'S EXTRAORDINARY LOVE

Now place God in the moment with you.
What is His role in the scene?

What is God trying to reveal to you about His love?

God, I thank you for the gift of extraordinary love in my ordinary life.
Please help me to continuously seek your heart and recognize the
blessing of your presence all around me.

AMEN.

MY ORDINARY MOMENT

Describe the moment as it happened.

What emotions are surfacing?
What about the experience do you feel called to ponder more deeply?

_____/_____/_____

GOD'S EXTRAORDINARY LOVE

Now place God in the moment with you.
What is His role in the scene?

What is God trying to reveal to you about His love?

God, I thank you for the gift of extraordinary love in my ordinary life.
Please help me to continuously seek your heart and recognize the
blessing of your presence all around me.

AMEN.

MY ORDINARY MOMENT

Describe the moment as it happened.

What emotions are surfacing?
What about the experience do you feel called to ponder more deeply?

_____ / _____ / _____

GOD'S EXTRAORDINARY LOVE

Now place God in the moment with you.
What is His role in the scene?

What is God trying to reveal to you about His love?

God, I thank you for the gift of extraordinary love in my ordinary life.
Please help me to continuously seek your heart and recognize the
blessing of your presence all around me.

AMEN.

MY ORDINARY MOMENT

Describe the moment as it happened.

What emotions are surfacing?
What about the experience do you feel called to ponder more deeply?

_____/_____/_____

Now place God in the moment with you.
What is His role in the scene?

What is God trying to reveal to you about His love?

God, I thank you for the gift of extraordinary love in my ordinary life.
Please help me to continuously seek your heart and recognize the
blessing of your presence all around me.

AMEN.

MY ORDINARY MOMENT

Describe the moment as it happened.

What emotions are surfacing?
What about the experience do you feel called to ponder more deeply?

_____ / _____ / _____

GOD'S EXTRAORDINARY LOVE

Now place God in the moment with you.
What is His role in the scene?

What is God trying to reveal to you about His love?

God, I thank you for the gift of extraordinary love in my ordinary life.
Please help me to continuously seek your heart and recognize the
blessing of your presence all around me.

AMEN.

MY ORDINARY MOMENT

Describe the moment as it happened.

What emotions are surfacing?
What about the experience do you feel called to ponder more deeply?

_____ / _____ / _____

GOD'S EXTRAORDINARY LOVE

Now place God in the moment with you.
What is His role in the scene?

What is God trying to reveal to you about His love?

God, I thank you for the gift of extraordinary love in my ordinary life.
Please help me to continuously seek your heart and recognize the
blessing of your presence all around me.

AMEN.

Describe the moment as it happened.

What emotions are surfacing?
What about the experience do you feel called to ponder more deeply?

_____ / _____ / _____

GOD'S EXTRAORDINARY LOVE

Now place God in the moment with you.
What is His role in the scene?

What is God trying to reveal to you about His love?

God, I thank you for the gift of extraordinary love in my ordinary life.
Please help me to continuously seek your heart and recognize the
blessing of your presence all around me.

AMEN.

MY ORDINARY MOMENT

Describe the moment as it happened.

What emotions are surfacing?
What about the experience do you feel called to ponder more deeply?

/   /

GOD'S EXTRAORDINARY LOVE

Now place God in the moment with you.
What is His role in the scene?

What is God trying to reveal to you about His love?

God, I thank you for the gift of extraordinary love in my ordinary life.
Please help me to continuously seek your heart and recognize the
blessing of your presence all around me.

AMEN.

MY ORDINARY MOMENT

Describe the moment as it happened.

What emotions are surfacing?
What about the experience do you feel called to ponder more deeply?

_____/_____/_____

GOD'S EXTRAORDINARY LOVE

Now place God in the moment with you.
What is His role in the scene?

What is God trying to reveal to you about His love?

God, I thank you for the gift of extraordinary love in my ordinary life.
Please help me to continuously seek your heart and recognize the
blessing of your presence all around me.

AMEN.

MY ORDINARY MOMENT

Describe the moment as it happened.

What emotions are surfacing?
What about the experience do you feel called to ponder more deeply?

___/___/___

GOD'S EXTRAORDINARY LOVE

Now place God in the moment with you.
What is His role in the scene?

What is God trying to reveal to you about His love?

God, I thank you for the gift of extraordinary love in my ordinary life.
Please help me to continuously seek your heart and recognize the
blessing of your presence all around me.

AMEN.

MY ORDINARY MOMENT

Describe the moment as it happened.

What emotions are surfacing?
What about the experience do you feel called to ponder more deeply?

_____ / _____ / _____

GOD'S EXTRAORDINARY LOVE

Now place God in the moment with you.
What is His role in the scene?

What is God trying to reveal to you about His love?

God, I thank you for the gift of extraordinary love in my ordinary life.
Please help me to continuously seek your heart and recognize the
blessing of your presence all around me.

AMEN.

MY ORDINARY MOMENT

Describe the moment as it happened.

What emotions are surfacing?
What about the experience do you feel called to ponder more deeply?

_____/_____/_____

GOD'S EXTRAORDINARY LOVE

Now place God in the moment with you.
What is His role in the scene?

What is God trying to reveal to you about His love?

God, I thank you for the gift of extraordinary love in my ordinary life.
Please help me to continuously seek your heart and recognize the
blessing of your presence all around me.

AMEN.

MY ORDINARY MOMENT

Describe the moment as it happened.

What emotions are surfacing?
What about the experience do you feel called to ponder more deeply?

_____/_____/_____

GOD'S EXTRAORDINARY LOVE

Now place God in the moment with you.
What is His role in the scene?

What is God trying to reveal to you about His love?

God, I thank you for the gift of extraordinary love in my ordinary life.
Please help me to continuously seek your heart and recognize the
blessing of your presence all around me.

AMEN.

MY ORDINARY MOMENT

Describe the moment as it happened.

What emotions are surfacing?
What about the experience do you feel called to ponder more deeply?

_____/_____/_____

GOD'S EXTRAORDINARY LOVE

Now place God in the moment with you.
What is His role in the scene?

What is God trying to reveal to you about His love?

God, I thank you for the gift of extraordinary love in my ordinary life.
Please help me to continuously seek your heart and recognize the
blessing of your presence all around me.

AMEN.

MY ORDINARY MOMENT

Describe the moment as it happened.

What emotions are surfacing?
What about the experience do you feel called to ponder more deeply?

_____/_____/_____

Now place God in the moment with you.
What is His role in the scene?

What is God trying to reveal to you about His love?

God, I thank you for the gift of extraordinary love in my ordinary life.
Please help me to continuously seek your heart and recognize the
blessing of your presence all around me.

AMEN.

MY ORDINARY MOMENT

Describe the moment as it happened.

What emotions are surfacing?
What about the experience do you feel called to ponder more deeply?

_____ / _____ / _____

GOD'S EXTRAORDINARY LOVE

Now place God in the moment with you.
What is His role in the scene?

What is God trying to reveal to you about His love?

God, I thank you for the gift of extraordinary love in my ordinary life.
Please help me to continuously seek your heart and recognize the
blessing of your presence all around me.

AMEN.

Describe the moment as it happened.

What emotions are surfacing?
What about the experience do you feel called to ponder more deeply?

_____ / _____ / _____

GOD'S EXTRAORDINARY LOVE

Now place God in the moment with you.
What is His role in the scene?

What is God trying to reveal to you about His love?

God, I thank you for the gift of extraordinary love in my ordinary life.
Please help me to continuously seek your heart and recognize the
blessing of your presence all around me.

AMEN.

From there
you will seek
the Lord your God,
and you will find him
if you search
after him
with all your
heart and soul.

Deuteronomy 4:29

ON SILENCE

Silence is the beginning of purifying the soul.
- St. Basil the Great

Preparing your mind and heart for prayer and staying focused during prayer can be quite a challenge! Our culture bombards us with constant noise and activity, but our faith shows us another way. We need silence in order to reflect and grow in our walk with God.

Here are a few suggestions to help you quiet down and enter into prayer:

Turn off the technology around you.

In this digital age, we're surrounded by constant distractions. Try turning your phone on silent and putting it away someplace where you can't see it. The less you can see and hear your phone, the less you'll be distracted by dinging notifications or text messages!

Find a quiet place to pray.

Though praying at church or during adoration is beautiful and always highly recommended, it isn't always possible to get there. That's okay! The most important thing is that you have a place where you can clear your mind and focus. A few ideas include a chair in a corner, the porch or patio, a blanket in the grass, in your bed, in your car, on a park bench, or at the kitchen table first thing in the morning.

Be in nature.

God often speaks to us through the things he has created, so surrounding yourself with nature can help you to enter into prayer. Don't be afraid to get outside! Praying on the top of a mountain, at the beach, or even in your own backyard or garden can be a very spiritually rich experience.

Write down your to-do list or your worries.

If you have a long to-do list or anything else weighing on you mentally, jot those items down on a piece of paper and set it to the side for later. Surrender your worries to the Lord.

Make a prayer routine.

Sometimes having a specific routine that you do every time you pray can help you to clear your mind and relax into prayer. This routine can be simple or elaborate; whatever works for you! Consider lighting a candle, getting out your Bible (even if you just hold it), or snuggling up in a cozy blanket. Doing the same action every time helps you to associate prayerful quiet with your time with God.

Practice slow breathing.

Sit quietly and just breathe for 2-3 minutes. Focus on your breath softly flowing in and out as you clear your mind. If your focus begins to wander, you can whisper the name of Jesus over and over. This process may be a struggle at first, but take heart! Practice makes perfect. The first few times you sit quietly, the silence may seem deafening, but the more you practice sitting in silence, the easier it will become.

YOUR
BOOKMARK

Please use this bookmark as you
pray though your journal.

Cut along the dashed line and
fold in half horizontally. Place
folded bookmark over your
current page.

O God,
help me
to seek
your face
throughout
each moment
of this day.
Help me to
serve you
with a
humble and
grateful heart.

Amen.

CONNECT

www.livetodaywellco.com

Instagram @livetodaywellco

facebook.com/livetodaywellco

#theseekjournal #livetodaywellco

live today well

COLLECTIVE

Made in the USA
Coppell, TX
12 February 2020